EARTH ONE

Written by **Geoff Johns**

Pencils by **Gary Frank**

Inks by **Jonathan Sibal**

Color by **Brad Anderson**

Lettered by **Rob Leigh**

Batman created by **Bob Kane**

DEDICATIONS

For his shining gentle spirit and the light it cast all around him. This book is dedicated to the memory of our beloved archivist Roger Bonas. He was the guardian of DC's past and he will forever be part of its legacy.

— **Geoff Johns**

For Ian Meek.
A great friend, an inspiration to many and walking proof that adversity can lead some men to become heroes.

— **Gary Frank**

Eddie Berganza Editor – Original Series
Darren Shan Assistant Editor – Original Series
Jeb Woodard Group Editor – Collected Editions
Curtis King Jr. Publication Design

Bob Harras Senior VP – Editor-in-Chief, DC Comics

Diane Nelson President
Dan DiDio and **Jim Lee** Co-Publishers
Geoff Johns Chief Creative Officer
Amit Desai Senior VP – Marketing & Global Franchise Management
Nairi Gardiner Senior VP – Finance
Sam Ades VP – Digital Marketing
Bobbie Chase VP – Talent Development
Mark Chiarello Senior VP – Art, Design & Collected Editions
John Cunningham VP – Content Strategy
Anne DePies VP – Strategy Planning & Reporting
Don Falletti VP – Manufacturing Operations
Lawrence Ganem VP – Editorial Administration & Talent Relations
Alison Gill Senior VP – Manufacturing & Operations
Hank Kanalz Senior VP – Editorial Strategy & Administration
Jay Kogan VP – Business Affairs
Derek Maddalena Senior VP – Sales & Business Development
Jack Mahan VP – Business Affairs
Dan Miron VP – Sales Planning & Trade Development
Nick Napolitano VP – Manufacturing Administration
Carol Roeder VP – Marketing
Eddie Scannell VP – Mass Account & Digital Sales
Courtney Simmons Senior VP – Publicity & Communicationsy
Jim (Ski) Sokolowski VP – Comic Book Specialty & Newsstand Sales
Sandy Yi Senior VP – Global Franchise Management

BATMAN: EARTH ONE

DC Comics, 4000 Warner Blvd., Burbank, CA 91522.
A Warner Bros. Entertainment Company
Printed by RR Donnelley, Salem, VA, USA. 8/28/15. Second Printing.
ISBN: 978-1-4012-3209-2

PEFC Certified

Printed on paper from sustainably managed forests and controlled sources

PEFC/29-31-75   www.pefc.org

Library of Congress Cataloging-in-Publication Data

Johns, Geoff, 1973-
  Batman : earth one / Geoff Johns, Gary Frank.
  p. cm.
  ISBN 978-1-4012-3208-5 -- ISBN 978-1-4012-3209-2
  1. Graphic novels. I. Frank, Gary, 1969- II. Title.
PN6728.B36J64 2012
741.5'973--dc23
                                    2012000608

NOW.

CLKK

KLAK

THEN.

YOU NEED SOME HELP GETTIN' OUT, PAL?

NO.

TINK

Tt.

THOMAS WAYNE ★ FOR ★ MAYOR

A NORMAL LIFE? IN THIS MANSION? WITH BUTLERS, MAIDS AND COOKS?

THIS *ISN'T* NORMAL, TOMMY. YOU DON'T KNOW WHAT NORMAL IS. BEING A WAYNE, YOU NEVER HAVE.

LIFE'S UGLY OUTSIDE THIS PALACE OF YOURS.

I *KNOW* HOW *UGLY* LIFE CAN BE.

AFTER EVERYTHING WE DID IN THE DESERT, I'LL *NEVER* FORGET THAT.

THEY'RE WAITING FOR ME.

TOMMY, I...

"WE'VE GOT A FRONT ROW SEAT!"

HEY.

WATCH WHERE YOU'RE GOIN', KID.

I DON'T HAVE TO DO *ANYTHING* YOU SAY.

MY PARENTS ARE THE *RICHEST* PEOPLE IN GOTHAM CITY.

YOU'RE THE WAYNE KID.

BRUCE?!

LEGAL GUARDIAN?

I'M NOT A PARENT.

ACCORDING TO THIS, YOU HAVE A DAUGHTER.

SHE LIVES WITH HER MOTHER.

IN SEOUL?

THAT'S NOT WHAT I MEANT WHEN I SAID I'M NOT A PARENT. I MEANT I'M NOT INTERESTED IN BEING ANYONE'S GUARDIAN.

I JUST WANT TO KNOW WHO KILLED THE WAYNES.

THAT'S THE POLICE'S JOB, MR. PENNYWORTH. MY JOB IS TO SORT OUT WHAT HAPPENS TO THIS POOR BOY.

HE WON'T TALK TO ANYONE. HE HASN'T EATEN ANYTHING.

THERE HAS TO BE SOMEONE ELSE WHO CAN WATCH OVER HIM.

THOMAS AND MARTHA WERE THE LAST OF THEIR RESPECTIVE FAMILIES. THE LAST OF THE WAYNES AND THE ARKHAMS.

WHAT HAPPENS IF I SAY "NO"?

HE GOES TO CHILD SERVICES.

AND INTO FOSTER CARE.

LOOK...
BRUCE...

WE'LL SEE IF WE CAN GET ANY PRINTS AS SOON AS WE GET A CHANCE.

WHO'S *NEXT?!* *NEXT!!*

HEY, DAD!

BUSY NIGHT, *huh?*

BARBARA?

I TOLD YOU NOT TO COME TO THE STATION AFTER DARK. AND IT'S A SCHOOL NIGHT--

YOU FORGOT DINNER.

I WASN'T HUNGRY.

IT'S LASAGNA.

MOM'S RECIPE.

YOU'LL SEE A BIOGRAPHY OF YOURS TRULY IN THE *BEHIND-THE-SCENES,* BUT HERE ARE THE *BULLETPOINTS:*

BORN AND RAISED IN LOS ANGELES. SPENT NINE YEARS WORKING HOMICIDE FOR HOLLYWOOD P.D. PALM TREES. BEACHES. GIRLS.

MORE GIRLS.

Hm.

WEST COAST IS A BEAUTIFUL PLACE...

BUT I'M BEGINNING TO SEE *GOTHAM* HAS ITS BEAUTY *TOO.*

HI, YOURSELF, SWEETHEART.

WHO IN THEIR RIGHT MIND TRANSFERS TO GOTHAM?

I NEEDED A NEW CHALLENGE. GOTHAM IS THE MOST DANGEROUS CITY IN AMERICA. EVERY CRIME IN GOTHAM IS A POTENTIAL *HEADLINE*.

I *LIKE* HEADLINES. IN FACT, I'M GOING TO TACKLE *ONE* CASE IN PARTICULAR THAT WENT COLD *YEARS* AGO.

THE MURDERS OF THOMAS AND MARTHA WAYNE.

SOLVE *THAT* DIAMOND IN THE ROUGH?

IT'S OUT OF *TELEVISION* AND INTO *FILM*.

WAYNE, THOMAS

ARKHAM-WAYNE, MARTHA

WHY A *BAT?*

BECAUSE OF THE DAY YOU OPENED THE MAUSOLEUM? YOU THINK PEOPLE WILL BE AS SCARED AS YOU WERE?

THE KIND OF PEOPLE YOU'RE HUNTING *DON'T* GET SCARED.

EVERYONE GETS SCARED, ALFRED.

"THERE'RE TWO SIDES TO EVERYTHING, BRUCE!"

THE WAYNE
MEDICAL GROUP

THE FOX HOLE

EXCUSE ME,
MR. FOX.

YOU... YOU'RE BRUCE WAYNE.

YES.

ARE YOU LOOKING FOR THE WAYNE BOARDROOM? IT'S, *uh*, IT'S ON THE TOP FLOOR.

THIS IS DESIGN AND ENGINEERING.

I KNOW.

DID I DO SOMETHING WRONG? AM I FIRED? I SWEAR I DIDN'T THINK THE SPOT WAS *RESERVED*. YOU HAVEN'T EVER PARKED THERE, SO I THOUGHT--

I NEED YOU TO DO SOMETHING FOR ME.

YOU WERE THE LEAD DESIGNER ON THE NEUROPROSTHETICS PROCESSOR.

I WAS, BUT DOCTOR HABERMAN TOOK THAT OVER. IT ULTIMATELY DIDN'T INTEGRATE WITH THE NERVOUS SYSTEM. IT WAS SCRAPPED.

AND HE SCRAPPED YOU TOO AFTER YOU BROKE HIS NOSE.

MY...PASSION GOT THE BETTER OF ME. AXONS MYELINATION IS POSSIBLE. PERMANENT ARTIFICIAL LIMBS ARE THE FUTURE. I BELIEVE THAT EVEN IF HE DOESN'T.

IF YOU HELP ME, I'LL SEE THAT YOU'RE PUT BACK ON THE PROJECT. AND THAT YOUR FIVE-YEAR-OLD NIECE IS THE FIRST TO RECEIVE ONE. SHE LOST HER ARM IN AN ACCIDENT, DIDN'T SHE?

WHAT *EXACTLY* DO YOU WANT ME TO *DO*, MR. WAYNE?

I WANT YOU TO KEEP THIS BETWEEN US.

HERE.

WHAT IS IT?

I USE IT FOR MOUNTAIN CLIMBING.

CAN YOU FIX IT?

MR. WAYNE, WE WORK IN *MEDICAL* TECHNOLOGY--

CAN YOU FIX IT?

WELL, YES, BUT...MOUNTAIN CLIMBING?

MR. WAYNE?

MR. WAYNE, THERE'RE NO MOUNTAINS TO CLIMB IN GOTHAM CITY!

SURE THERE ARE.

WHAT THAT PUNK OWED ME IS COMIN' FROM YOU, GORDON.

AND YOU BETTER LEARN THE *RULES* OF GOTHAM, NEW GUY.

OR WE'LL SEE WHO'S *REALLY* STUPID.

WHAT THE HELL WAS *THAT?*

IS HE GREASING YOU?

JUST GET IN THE CAR, BULLOCK.

YOU DON'T KNOW WHAT YOU'RE TALKING ABOUT.

I'M NOT *BLIND*, GORDO.

DON'T *LECTURE* ME FROM SOME FICTIONAL MORAL *HIGH HORSE* AS IF YOU'VE COME HERE FOR ANY OTHER REASON THAN *PUBLICITY* AND *SELF-PROMOTION*.

AS SOON AS YOU HIT THE SAME WALL EVERYONE ELSE HAS TRYING TO SOLVE THE MURDERS OF THE WAYNES, YOU'LL BE ON THE FIRST PLANE BACK TO LOS ANGELES.

AND I'LL BUY THE TICKET.

DON'T JUDGE ME, BULLOCK. YOU DON'T *KNOW* ME.

MR. WAYNE!

OH, MR. WAYNE!

EXCUSE ME.

CHK

WHERE'D HE GO?

"JUST DO IT *QUIETLY*."

NICE LIGHTER.

NNFFF!

WHERE'D YOU GET IT, SCUMBAG?

"AND WE'LL TAKE CARE OF *TWO BIRDS* WITH *ONE STONE*."

I ASKED YOU TO GET JESSICA DENT OFF MY BACK, JUDGE PATTERSON. YOU DIDN'T.

I DON'T LIKE EXCUSES. DO WHAT I ASK OR YOUR YOUNGEST DAUGHTER IS NEXT.

I'LL TELL YOUR OLDEST *GOODBYE*.

Kk.

Wkk.

Mm.

YES. VERY NICE.

OH.

HE'LL LIKE YOU.

TELL HIM TO HURRY UP WITH HER.

I WANT JACOB WEAVER TAKEN CARE OF TONIGHT.

WKK.

HOW'S THE NOSE?

DON'T YOU HAVE SOME PAPERWORK TO FILL OUT?

WHAT PAPERWORK?

ON "BATMAN"?

OH, COME ON.

THE MAYOR ALREADY CALLED THE COMMISSIONER WHO CALLED THE CAPTAIN. THEY WANT TO KNOW WHO THE HELL HE IS.

SOME *NUT* LOOKING FOR *ATTENTION.*

TAKES ONE TO KNOW ONE, I GUESS.

HEY! WHERE ARE YOU GOING?

SHIFT'S OVER, BULLOCK.

I'M GOING *HOME.*

EXCUSE ME, GORGEOUS.

WHERE DO THEY KEEP THE *COLD CASES* AROUND HERE?

HEY THERE, DOLL. I WANT TO CHECK OUT SOME FILES.

THE WAYNE CASE. AS IN THOMAS AND MARTHA.

AND YOU ARE?

DETECTIVE HARVEY BULLOCK. JUST JOINED THE PRECINCT.

BULLOCK...

YOU'RE NOT ON MY LIST YET, DETECTIVE.

WHAT'S THAT MEAN?

THAT MEANS I CAN'T GIVE YOU ANYTHING UNTIL YOU ARE. PAPERWORK IS PROBABLY STILL ROUTING.

SO?

CHECK BACK TOMORROW.

OH, NO.

BARBARA?

I'M SORRY I'M LATE.

...BARBARA?

BZZD

HELLO?

HEY, DAD.

BARBARA? WHERE ARE YOU?

LEAVING THE LIBRARY.

HELENA CALLED IN SICK AGAIN. I THOUGHT I COULD USE THE EXTRA SHIFT.

WHAT HAVE WE TALKED ABOUT? I DON'T WANT YOU OUT AFTER DARK.

THE RENT CHECK BOUNCED AGAIN.

...BARBARA, I...

DON'T WORRY ABOUT IT, DAD.

WE'RE IN THIS TOGETHER.

THUMP
THUMP
THUMP

NICE APRON.

WHAT ARE YOU DOING HERE?

I'VE GOT TO TALK TO YOU, GORDO.

YOU KNOW THAT BAT-GUY WHO WAS HARASSING JACOB WEAVER?

YOU FORGET YOUR KEYS AGAIN?

WEAVER WAS THE *FIRST* COP ON THE SCENE OF THE WAYNE MURDER.

AND NOW WEAVER'S *DEAD*.

LANDLADY JUST FOUND HIM WITH HIS *THROAT* SLASHED. THEY'RE ACTUALLY TRYING TO CALL IT A *SUICIDE*.

GET THE HELL OUT OF MY HOME, BULLOCK.

GORDO, WHATEVER'S HAPPENING... I DON'T KNOW IF IT'S CONNECTED TO THE WAYNES OR BAT-GUY OR THE MAYOR, BUT IT'S *SOMETHING BIG*.

I KNOW WHEN A *HEADLINE'S* BREWING. I CAN *SMELL* IT.

BZZD

BARBAR

CASE

BARBARA?

NO, DETECTIVE GORDON.

AXE?! WHAT ARE YOU DOING WITH MY *DAUGHTER'S* PHONE? WHERE *IS* SHE?!

SOMEWHERE. BUT NOT EXACTLY SOMEWHERE *SAFE*.

THAT'S UP TO *YOU*.

YOU WERE WARNED BEFORE TO STAY OUT OF THE ARCHIVES--TO NOT DIG WHERE PEOPLE DON'T *WANT* YOU TO.

YOU CHECKED OUT SOME FILES TODAY. YOU WANT TO SEE YOUR DAUGHTER AGAIN; YOU *PUT THEM BACK*.

WHAT? WHAT *IS* IT

WHERE YOU GOIN', HONEYS?

WE GOTTA GO TO WORK.

I'VE GOT WORK FOR YOU, BABY.

COME BACK!

KRAK

GORDON?

YOU'RE GOING TO TELL ME WHERE MY DAUGHTER IS.

YOU DON'T--

--AND THERE'LL BE TROUBLE.

WHAT IS THIS SUPPOSED TO BE?

GOOD COP, BAD COP?

C'MON, AXE. I GET IT NOW. THIS IS GOTHAM CITY.

HELP!

"PROMISE ME YOU'LL *NEVER* GO INSIDE, OKAY?"

"*BAD THINGS* HAPPENED HERE."

KRRATTCH

THWAM

AAH.

WHAT *IS* THAT? WHAT...

KLK

BULLOCK?

WE TOOK THAT PSYCHO DOWN. BATMAN CUFFED HIM IN THERE AND LEFT. SAID HE WAS GOING TO TALK TO HIS BOSS. I'M GUESSING COBBLEPOT.

GORDON, YOUR DAUGHTER WASN'T THE FIRST GIRL HE ATTACKED...

...I'VE GOT TO... I'VE GOT TO CALL THIS IN.

BULLOCK--?

I'M FINE.

HOW DID YOU KNOW I WAS HERE, DAD?

LET ME OUTTA HERE!

FWUMP FWUMP

I'M SO SORRY, BARBARA.

WILL YOU STOP ALWAYS SAYING THAT?

STOP BLAMING YOURSELF.

HOW'D YOU GET SO NICE?

I TAKE AFTER MOM.

I SAID I WAS SORRY!

"VENGEANCE"? HAHAHAHAHA! HOW DRAMATIC.

KRAK

YOU'VE SPENT YEARS GETTING FAT AND RICH OFF THE PEOPLE OF GOTHAM. IT COULD'VE BEEN DIFFERENT.

IT SHOULD HAVE BEEN.

AAAKK!

COME ON, BRUCE. COME ON.

DON'T GO ANYWHERE.

STAY WITH ME.

ALFRED...

LET'S GET YOU HOME.

EEP

THE DEATH OF MAYOR OSWALD COBBLEPOT WAS A SHOCK IN ITSELF, BUT THE AMOUNT OF INFORMATION COMING TO LIGHT ABOUT HIS ILLEGAL AND CORRUPT ACTIVITIES IS STAGGERING.

THE MOST HEINOUS BEING THE ACTUAL *EMPLOYMENT* OF A SERIAL KILLER WHO RECENTLY ESCAPED FROM THE CRANE INSTITUTE.

RAY SALINGER IS BETTER KNOWN AS *THE BIRTHDAY BOY*, A SERIAL KILLER FASCINATED WITH YOUNG GIRLS RESEMBLING HIS FIRST VICTIM, 15-YEAR-OLD DEBUTANTE AMANDA GRANT.

A MEMBER OF THE GOTHAM CITY POLICE DEPARTMENT WISHING TO REMAIN ANONYMOUS CLAIMS THAT *BATMAN* IS RESPONSIBLE FOR BOTH THE *CAPTURE* OF THE BIRTHDAY BOY *AND* THE *DEATH* OF MAYOR COBBLEPOT.

THE POLICE CHIEF HAS REFUSED TO VERIFY IF BATMAN *IS* INVOLVED OR WHO THEY SUSPECT THIS VIGILANTE TO REALLY BE.

EARLIER THIS AFTERNOON, THE PRESIDENT OF THE BOARD OF SUPERVISORS, JESSICA DENT, WAS SWORN IN AS THE NEW MAYOR OF GOTHAM CITY.

MISS DENT, TWIN SISTER TO D.A. HARVEY DENT, IS A WELL-KNOWN FIGURE IN GOTHAM, MOST RECENTLY RESPONSIBLE FOR THE CLEANUP PROJECT ON THE EAST SIDE AND MOST FAMOUS FOR HER STRING OF CLASHES WITH COBBLEPOT.

GOTHAM CITY IS *CHANGING*.

LET'S HOPE IT'S FOR THE BETTER.

COOL.

WHAT CAN I GET YOU, PAL?

IT WAS JUST THE WRONG ALLEY AT THE WRONG TIME.

THERE *WAS* NO CONSPIRACY, BRUCE. IT WAS A STUPID, RANDOM ROBBERY.

SO NOW YOU CAN PUT AWAY THAT *COSTUME.*

NOW YOU CAN *STOP.*

NO, ALFRED.

NOW I CAN *NEVER* STOP.

NOW I'LL ALWAYS BE ALONE.

BRUCE...

GEOFF JOHNS is one of the most prolific and popular contemporary comic book writers. He has written highly acclaimed stories starring Superman, Green Lantern, the Flash, Teen Titans, and Justice Society of America. He is the author of the *New York Times* best-selling graphic novels GREEN LANTERN: RAGE OF THE RED LANTERNS, GREEN LANTERN: SINESTRO CORPS WAR, JUSTICE SOCIETY OF AMERICA: THY KINGDOM COME, SUPERMAN: BRAINIAC and BLACKEST NIGHT.

Johns was born in Detroit and studied media arts, screenwriting, film production and film theory at Michigan State University. After moving to Los Angeles, he worked as an intern and later an assistant for film director Richard Donner, whose credits include *Superman: The Movie*, *Lethal Weapon 4* and *Conspiracy Theory*.

Johns began his comics career writing STARS AND S.T.R.I.P.E. and creating Stargirl for DC Comics. He received the Wizard Fan Award for Breakout Talent of 2002 and Writer of the Year for 2005, 2006, 2007 and 2008 as well as the CBG Writer of the Year 2003 through 2005 and 2007 and 2008, and CBG Best Comic Book Series for JSA 2001 through 2005.

After acclaimed runs on THE FLASH, TEEN TITANS and the best-selling INFINITE CRISIS miniseries, Johns co-wrote a run on ACTION COMICS with his mentor Donner. In 2006, he co-wrote 52, an ambitious weekly comic book series set in real time, with Grant Morrison, Greg Rucka and Mark Waid. Johns has also written for various other media, including the acclaimed "Legion" episode of SMALLVILLE and the fourth season of ROBOT CHICKEN. He is writing the story of the DC Universe Online massively multiplayer action game from Sony Online Entertainment LLC and recently joined DC Entertainment as its Chief Creative Officer.

Johns currently resides in Los Angeles, California.

GARY FRANK, a native of Bristol, England, began his comics career working on various titles for Marvel UK before entering the American comics scene as the penciller on Marvel's *Incredible Hulk*. Frank then came to DC Comics where he was the original artist on BIRDS OF PREY and pencilled the adventures of SUPERGIRL. He has also worked on WildStorm's GEN 13 as well as his creator-owned series *The Kin*.

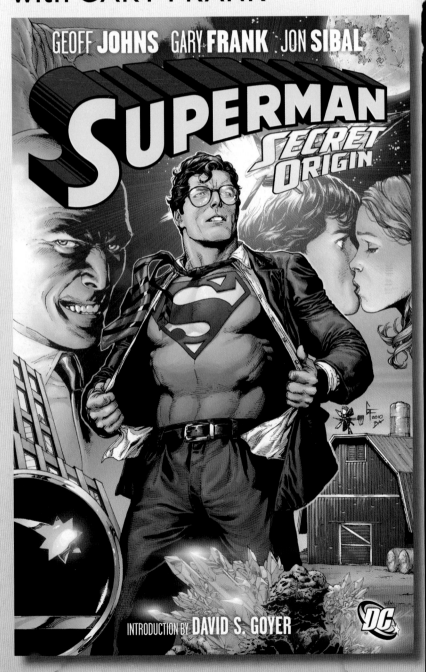